Blessings
And
Peaceful Promises

Blessings
And
Peaceful Promises

Dr. Delicia Walker

ISBN 978-1-957582-85-6 (paperback)
ISBN 978-1-957582-84-9 (eBook)

Printed in the United States of America

I extend my sincere thanks to my mom, Sheila Farquharson, grandparents: Wilhelmena Farquharson(deceased), Uellen Williams, family and friends for their love and continued support. Also, I extend my deepest gratitude to my husband Pastor Anthony Walker for his invaluable contributions and supporting my efforts.

Thank you

1

My Prayer For You

I *pray that these devotional scriptures lead you into a loving and spiritual relationship with* **Jesus Christ.**

Knowing God is a comfort to our hearts. Having a relationship with God can bring peace and harmony in our lives and provide deeper connections with Him and produce quality human interactions.

God can empower us to develop healthy relationships with others. As we practice and demonstrate a love for others, and incorporate a selflessness attitude, our relationships will improve and become pleasing and acceptable to God.

> ²⁰ *FOR ALL THE PROMISES OF GOD IN HIM ARE YEA, AND IN HIM AMEN, UNTO THE GLORY OF GOD BY US.*
> **2 Corinthians 1:20 KJV**

My God will Supply all your Needs according to His Riches in glory by Christ Jesus

Philippians 4:19

Faith
as a grain of mustard seed

³⁰ And he said, Whereunto shall we liken the kingdom of God? Or with what comparison shall we compare it? ³¹ It is like a grain of mustard seed, which, when it is sown in the earth, is less than all the seeds that be in the earth: ³² But when it is sown, it groweth up, and becometh greater than all herbs, and shooteth out great branches; so that the fowls of the air may lodge under the shadow of it.

Mark 4:30-32 KJV

Peace

```
L W B J X Z E N E R E S Y O I
W U S S E N T E I U Q J T A R
B X F X K H A R M O N Y I T I
U I X E N H T Q S B H R L R X
R Z Y J C U X T Q D R K I S R
L F N T H A I O M N D S U W F
N M Y C S L E N K L C S Q J G
Z E I O L T O P P F D J N G W
B F J N P S C T G C J E A O P
B P E Y J E Q O A F C J R O L
A S L I L R J L M N W W T D H
S A M T Z A M O E F L U Z W G
C O N T E N T L Y T O T W I P
L E X K E W I N G A V R P L B
G B D A G S R K Q L E H T L Y
```

CALM	COMFORT	CONTENT
GENTLE	GOODWILL	HARMONY
JOY	LOVE	PEACEFUL
QUIETNESS	REST	SERENE
SILENCE	STILLNESS	TRANQUILITY

God sends the rain to water the growth in our lives.

¹⁴ So shall the knowledge of wisdom be unto thy soul: when thou hast found it, then there shall be a reward, and thy expectation shall not be cut off.
Proverbs 24:14 KJV

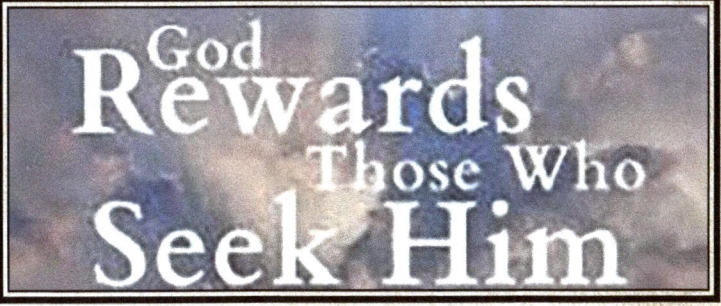

And the LORD God took the man, and put him into the garden of Eden to dress it and to keep it.

—Genesis 2:15

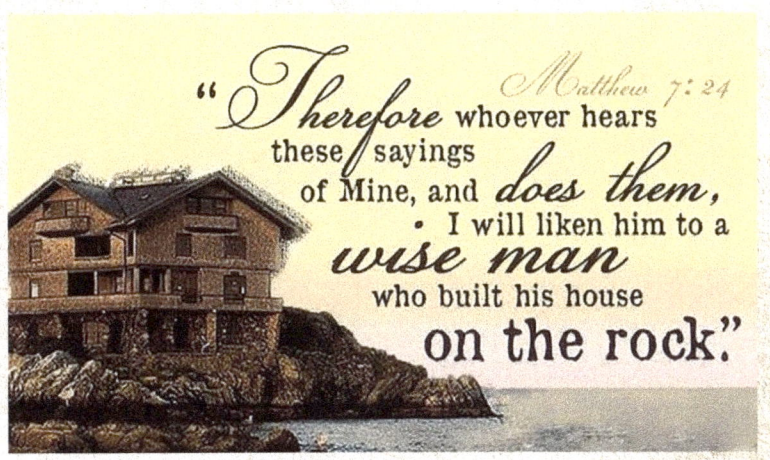

"*Therefore* whoever hears these sayings of Mine, and *does them,* • I will liken him to a *wise man* who built his house on the rock."

Matthew 7:24

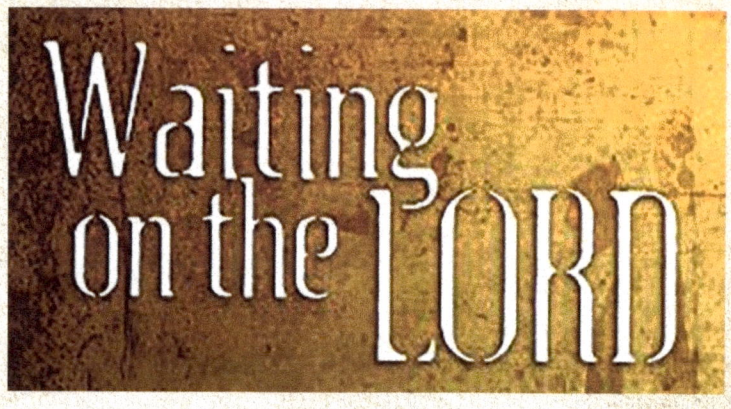

^{25} But if we hope for that we see not, then do we with patience wait for it.

Romans 8:25 KJV

¹¹ And the LORD shall guide thee continually,
and satisfy thy soul in drought, and
make fat thy bones: and thou shalt be
like a watered garden, and like a spring
of water, whose waters fail not.
Isaiah 58:11 KJV

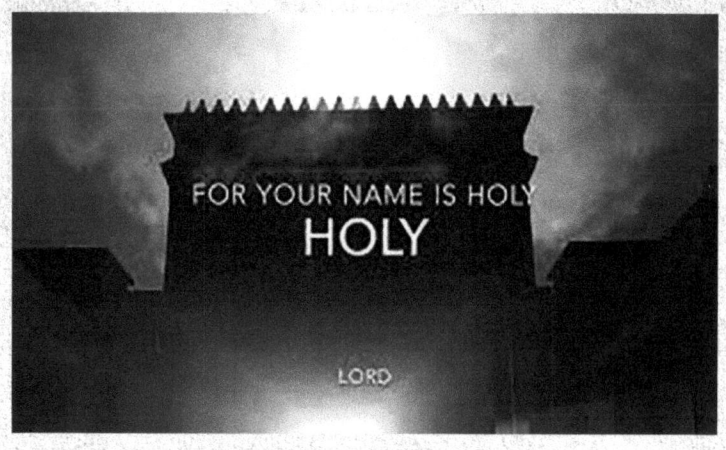

¹⁵ For thus saith the high and lofty One that
inhabiteth eternity, whose
name is Holy; I dwell
in the high and holy place, with him also that is
of a contrite and humble spirit, to revive the
spirit of the humble, and to
revive the heart of the
contrite ones.
Isaiah 57:15 KJV

God's timing is not ours. As we wait
upon Him to restore and guide our
lives, we develop trust, patience,
and faith knowing that He lives in
us and is working on our behalf.

God's Timing

> *Only God can keep all his promises.*

⁵⁶ Blessed be the LORD, that
hath given rest unto
his people Israel, according to all that he
promised: there hath not failed one word of all
his good promise, which he promised by the
hand of Moses his servant.
1 Kings 8:56 KJV

[38] For I am persuaded, that neither death, nor life, nor angels, nor principalities, nor powers, nor things present, nor things to come, [39] Nor height, nor depth, nor any other creature, shall be able to separate us from the love of God, which is in Christ Jesus our Lord.
Romans 8:38-39 KJV

¹⁴ And this is the confidence that we have in him, that, if we ask any thing according to his will, he heareth us: ¹⁵And if we know that he hear us, whatsoever we ask, we know that we have the petitions that we desired of him.
1 John 5:14-15 KJV

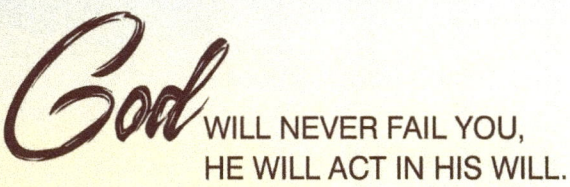

God WILL NEVER FAIL YOU,
HE WILL ACT IN HIS WILL.

[8] And the LORD, he it is that doth go
before thee; he will be with thee, he
will not fail thee, neither forsake thee:
fear not, neither be dismayed.
Deuteronomy 31:8 KJV

[9] If we confess our sins, he is faithful and just to forgive us our sins, and to cleanse us from all unrighteousness.
1 John 1:9 KJV

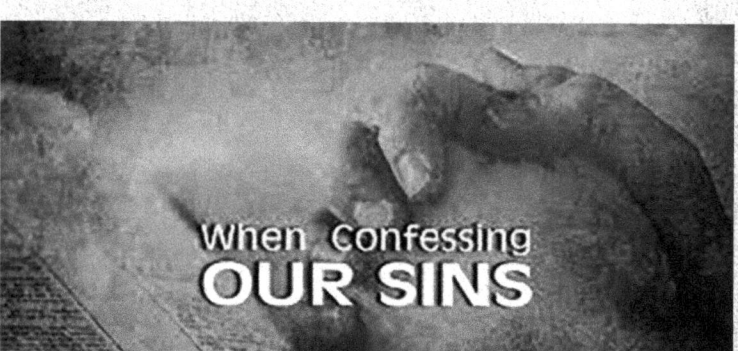

Fear thou not; for I am with thee: be not dismayed; for I am thy God: I will strengthen thee; yea, I will help thee; yea, I will uphold thee with the right hand of my righteousness.

Isaiah 41:10
King James Version

Believe

JOHN

I GIVE THEM ETERNAL
LIFE, AND THEY WILL
NEVER PERISH, AND
NO ONE WILL
SNATCH THEM OUT
of my hand.

10 : 28

The thief comes
only to steal and
kill and destroy.
I came that they
may have life and
have it abundantly.

–John 10:10

¹⁰ *Create* in me a *clean heart*, O God; and <u>Renew</u> a right *Spirit* within me.

Psalm 51:10 KJV

³ To every thing there is a season, and a time to every purpose under the heaven: Ecclesiastes 3:1 KJV

8 Draw nigh to God, and he will draw nigh to you. Cleanse your hands, ye sinners; and purify your hearts, ye doubled minded.

James 4:8 KJV

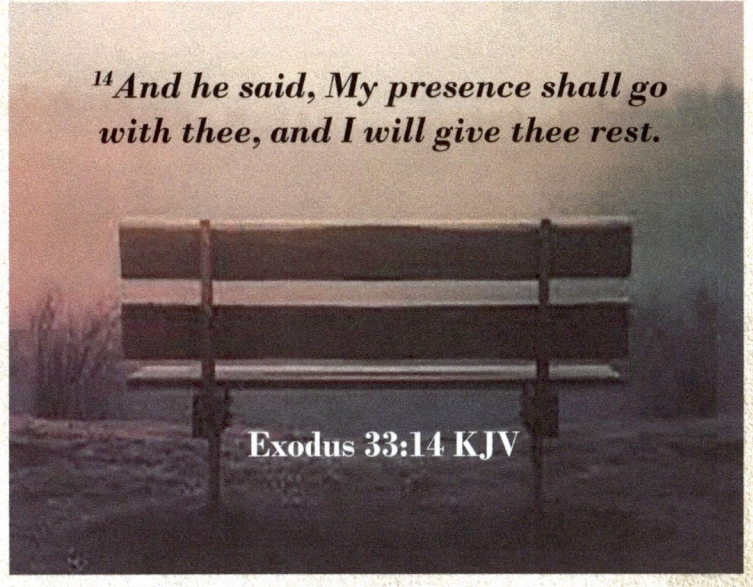

¹⁴*And he said, My presence shall go with thee, and I will give thee rest.*

Exodus 33:14 KJV

Dear
Anxiety,
Draw nearer
to God!

by Dr. Delicia Walker

Worry and anxiety can consume your inner
being…taking over your life and competing
for your time and attention. If not managed,
it can take over and become overwhelming.
Facing your anxiety and trusting God to deliver
you from fear can build stronger feelings and
inner peace that God can nurture and create a
deeper bond. Allow God to be in the Center of
your life. He will bless you beyond measure
in this moment. Draw nearer to Him!

¹³ *Those that be planted in the house of the Lord shall flourish in the courts of our God.*
Psalm 92:13 KJV

Give Thanks and

Praise Everyday!

8 He hath shewed thee, O man, what is good; and what doth the LORD require of thee, but to do justly, and to love mercy, and to walk humbly with thy God?
Micah 6:8 KJV

⁵ *But take diligent heed to do the commandment and the law, which Moses the servant of the LORD charged you, to love the LORD your God, and to walk in all his ways, and to keep his commandments, and to cleave unto him, and to serve him with all your heart and with all your soul.*

Joshua 22:5 KJV

¹¹ *For I know the thoughts that I think toward you, saith the LORD, thoughts of peace, and not of evil, to give you an expected end.*

Jeremiah 29:11 KJV

⁵ Who satisfieth thy mouth with good things;
so that thy youth is renewed like the eagle's.
Psalm 103:5 KJV

CALL TO **me** AND I WILL ANSWER **you** JEREMIAH 33:3

³Call unto me, and I will answer thee, and show thee great and mighty things, which thou knowest not.
Jeremiah 33:3 KJV

^{60} *Arise, shine; for thy light is come, and the glory of the LORD is risen upon thee.*
Isaiah 60:1 KJV

^{26} *But **Jesus** beheld them, and said unto them, With* men *this is* **IMPOSSIBLE**; *but with* **GOD** *all things are* **POSSIBLE**.

Matthew 19:26 KJV

God's Hands Are Safe

⁵ **Trust** in the **LORD** with all thine heart; and lean not unto thine own *understanding.* ⁶ In all thy ways **Acknowledge Him**, and **He** shall direct thy paths.
Proverbs 3:5-6 KJV

ASK, *and it shall be given you;*
SEEK, *and ye shall find;*
KNOCK, *and it shall be opened unto you:*

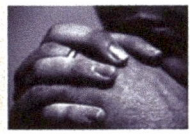  

Ask.   Seek.   Knock.

Matthew 7:7 KJV

Having a relationship with God is important for salvation for your life. He wants you to seek Him and His Word clarifies how to do it. God is the most important person in your life. The motivation should be to desire a deeper relationship with Him and focus on who He is. Seek the Lord and rest in Him.

¹⁷ *Therefore if any man be in Christ, he is a new creature: behold, all things are become new.*
2 Corinthians 5:17 KJV

Jesus Christ the same yesterday, and to day, and for ever.

Hebrews 13:8

ALL Things WORK TOGETHER for Good for those who Love GOD

ROMANS 8:28

GOD IS GOOD, ALL THE TIME.
ALL THE TIME, GOD IS GOOD.

[5] *For the **LORD** is good; his mercy is everlasting;*

*and his **truth** endureth to all generations.*

Psalm 100:5 KJV

"Mercy unto you, and peace, and love, be multiplied."
Jude 1:2
KJV

"Mercy unto you, and peace, and love, be multiplied."
Jude 1:2
KJV

¹⁵ For thus saith the Lord GOD, the Holy One of Israel; In returning and rest shall ye be saved; in quietness and in confidence shall be your strength: and ye would not.

Isaiah 30:15 KJV

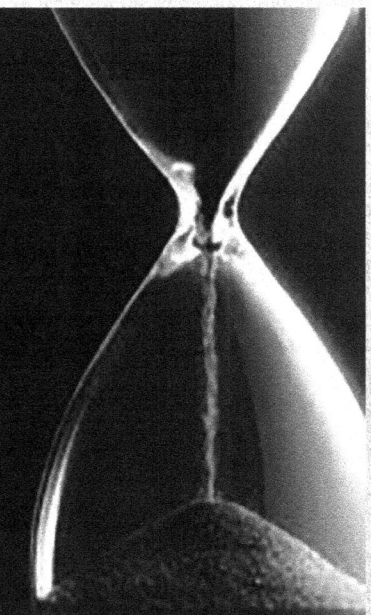

²³ But the hour cometh, and now is, when the true worshippers shall worship the Father in spirit and in truth: for the Father seeketh such to worship him. ²⁴ God is a Spirit: and they that worship him must worship him in spirit and in truth. **John 4: 23-24 KJV**

⁴ *Hear me when I call, O God of my righteousness: thou hast enlarged me when I was in distress; have mercy upon me, and hear my prayer.*

Psalm 4:1 KJV

Count your blessings and thank God for everything! God's gifts and riches of salvation can enrich your life and fill you with gratitude. God wants us to depend on Him as He alone can meet all our needs. Experiencing all the dimensions of God's blessings can deepen your spiritual relationship with Him.

1 2 3 4 5 6 7

² And the LORD answered me, and said, Write the vision, and make it plain upon tables, that he may run that readeth it.

Habakkuk 2:2 KJV

Notes

_____

_____

_____

_____

_____

_____

_____

_____

_____

_____

_____

_____

_____

_____

_____

_____

_____

About the Author

Dr. Delicia Walker is a writer, author, mentor, business professional, and a woman of faith. Her spiritual calling is to encourage, motivate, and inspire others. Dr. Walker's spiritual foundation in ministry has taken her through real life experiences, and reveals powerful testimonies through counseling of others, guidance, and her writings.

Delicia has also written the following books: *"Today You Are Loved,"* and *"Devotions From The Garden."*

Peace and Love Bestowed Upon You.

God's biblical principles and Scripture are vital for building a foundation that guides our lives. Being led by the Holy Spirit is necessary for recognizing what God is doing in your life. God knows what His children need to live, and He guides us through every circumstance of life. God wants us to trust Him, devote our time in prayer, and walk by faith. God is responsible for our future.